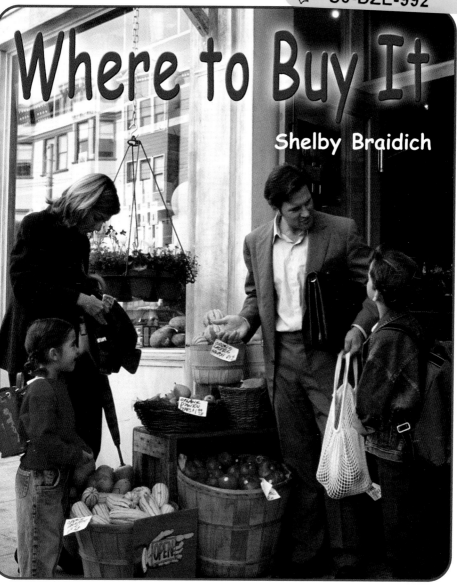

Where to Buy It

Shelby Braidich

Rosen
REAL
READERS

Rosen Classroom Books & Materials
New York

We buy milk at the store.

We buy oranges at the farmers market.

We buy a toy train at the toy store.

We buy a pizza at the pizza shop.

We buy candy at the candy shop.

We buy a fish at the pet store.

Words to Know

candy

fish

market

milk

oranges

pizza